PIECES OF MY MIND

Written by Riley Goldberg

Dedication:

This book is dedicated to my little sister. May you never have to experience the hardships I have. Remember, your heart is the fuel that runs your engine and your dreams are the scope that guides you.

Acknowledgement

I would like to say a deep thank you to my very best friends and my wonderful family who helped me throughout the tough times that inspired most of these works.

Table of Contents

Pieces of my mind

Places for my kind

If curiosity compels you

Take a step inside

-Riley Goldberg, *Pieces of My Mind*

Imagination:

Imagination

The minds' sweet plane

Sometimes it makes me

Feel insane.

Just sitting back to think

Can be quite a struggle

My mind floods like wetlands

My brain becomes a puddle.

But it's so great

To escape into the mindscape

To sit back in build

To wonder and create.

Stories, characters, worlds

All of them mine

Stories, characters, worlds

Yet reality, I can't find.

But it's alright,

I go on with my day

After all,

my mind is better anyway.

Who cares what I might miss

When I'm blessed by this bliss?

Who cares what I don't see

From this cruel reality?

I'm safe in my mind

This I truly know

I've said it before, I'll say it again

It's the best place to go.

Where I'm free to do anything

Where I'm happy. I'm happy.

Am I happy?

The truth is, yes

I am truly happy, yes.

I have a great life,

No reason to be depressed.

But just because I'm happy doesn't mean I'm not
stressed.

There's this fear that haunts me

Constantly

I'm terrified

That I'll lose my mind

And with it, all those who love me.

There is nothing I can do

To break away from the thought

That my imagination controls me

And will cause my mind to rot.

Everything I do contains a false reality

And I hate it but I love it. Why?

Oh please someone help me.

Even in my sleep

I retain no energy

Because my imagination doesn't stop

It goes on indefinitely.

Balance is what I need,

Between what is real and what I feel.

A balance I'm trying to find

To Provide liberation

A balance between reality and imagination.

6
Silent No Longer

Can't you hear my silent plea?

thought so loud, spoken silently

begging, pleading, to be set free

can't anyone hear my quiet plea?

I dare not use my real voice

in fear of retaliation

I have no real choice

Silence is my haven

Speak out, I must

to stop this madness

one once given trust

has brought me great sadness

To many souls
I share my story
But to trouble
I say I'm sorry.

that was before
I've changed as I should
no longer shall I stand for "jokes"
This madness stops for good.

My silent plea
will be silent no longer
for ways to fix this, I've long pondered
but help is my need
I shall no longer waunder

My plea will be heard

My thoughts have taken over

so now my plea is loud

Silent, no longer

The One Who I Despise

I often hear a voice

that echoes loud and clear.

It spews hurtful things

that I don't wish to hear.

It tells me many lies

that result in late-night cries.

But I know not who it is,

the one who I despise.

I've searched far and wide

for the voice's place of origin

I can never seem to find it

let it be known that I've tried

Nevertheless, it continues to speak

Many hurtful lies

That makes me feel weak.

I've searched for too long

I dare not deter

the search lasts forever

it becomes a blur.

Perhaps my search

is in vain

this tedious search

may provide no gain.

Though, upon consideration

Of the places I've looked

there is one nook,

and unchecked destination

that could prove to be

the voice's true location

But to my surprise

where the voice hides.

is within me

That's where it resides.

What should I do?

To rid myself of evil

to stop all the problems

to stop all the cries?

How do I get rid of

the one who I despise?

Early Bird, Late Bird

The early bird gets the worm

is an often-used term

The early bird eats alone

It's something to which she's prone

The early bird must be sad

She's got no friends to share her meal

but thou is just a bird

And sadness, she cannot feel.

One, who's not a bird,

wishes she could fly

but wonders, if she could,

to whom she'd say goodbye.

one fears she's much like

an early morning bird

who consumes food alone

and has none to share words

The early bird has no flock

she travels on her own

for she hasn't any time

to wait for those who are slow

The early bird must get tired

but she'd never let it show.

The early bird is a liar

But other birds can't know

13

The early bird is tired

the early bird is sad

the early bird is naught to anyone

no more than she is to herself.

This makes her feel bad

One is an Early bird,

who waits for others like her

however, this rare event

will never occur.

For there are no other early birds

who eat by themselves

at least none that'd be willing

to face One, herself.

The early bird

wishes to fly

far away

far and high

The earth below,

beckons her to fall

she dare not heed its persuasive call

for if she were to end it all

who'd be the early bird

who wakes each morning

to eat alone

a skill which she has honed

The early bird gets the worm

is an often-used term

The early bird gets a friend

only to lose it in the end

so what's the point of being early

if you lose all you like?

One, the early bird,

has pondered this her entire life

15

But she'll never find an answer

no matter how early she wakes

so she'll be constantly stuck

with the lies and the fakes.

No matter where she flies

How far, how high,

she'll never, *ever* escape

the late birds' cries.

Escape | Stress Is All We Know

Stress is all we know

No matter where we go

No one can be free

This is our reality

Nothing we can do

To stop this constant cycle

Stress, pressure, sleep

Will continue for a while

We say it's not bad

But we are in denial

Work, stress, and a large mess

Continuously piles

We need a break

A sweet escape

To make the stress

Dissipate.

Where can we go

To hide from this stress?

The mind is a place

One might suggest

Sit back and explore

The wonders of the mind

Wonders that others

Can't ever find.

A place of your own

Away from it all A

little paradise That

puts up a wall,

Blocking the outside

From that which is inside

All freedom, no rules

By which you must abide

The mind is a beautiful thing

It's the best place to go

Because the mind provides an escape

And stress is all we know.

Fear

A boy stands at a bus stop

A man does as well

The streets were wet

From when rain fell.

The man rubbed his eyes

And gave the boy a smile

"You know kid you're really lucky

To be a child."

The boy frowned

And asked the man why

The man just sighed

And looked to the sky.

"When you grow up

Life becomes a struggle.

Growing up sucks

It's nothing but trouble"

On that very day

The boy became afraid

From that day on

He'd be afraid

Of growing up

Of what the man said

I don't want to grow old

He thought to himself

I'll lose childhood, fun,

I could lose myself.

I'm afraid of what might happen

When I grow old I fear

That I may never be the same

As I was the previous year.

The boy locked himself away

To stay a child forever

He was not okay

Would he be okay ever?

A girl stands at a bus stop

A man does as well

The streets were wet

From when rain fell

The man looked at the girl

And gave her a smile.

"Growing up sucks.

I thought that for a while.

But really it's no different

Then being a child."

"Why is that?"

The young girl asked

As she twiddled her thumbs

And gave him a laugh

The man just sighed

And looked to the Sky.

"Ya know kid?

I don't actually know why…"

"…As a child all you can do

I have things done for you.

You sit back and watch

As there is nothing you can control

As an adult, you wander

around the earth

Hopelessly searching for something

That gives you worth.

Nobody cares about helping you out.

You lose your friends

All fun ends

The universe plays out

There's nothing you can do

All you can do is watch

As the world happens around you

No matter our age

We are all the same

So small, just pawns

In the universe's game.

So I don't complain.

Cause I'm just a guy standing at a bus stop

You're here as well

My mind is full

of tales to tell

So if you'll listen

If you'll choose to hear

I'll tell you that the future

is nothing to fear."

The Fixer

Are you happy?

Are they happy?

No, I don't feel crappy!

How could I feel bad, if everyone is happy?

Oh no please don't cry

I'll make it all better

I'll give you good advice

I'll clear the stormy weather

I'll be really nice

Be happy

Don't be mad

I'll fix it

I promise

You'll be glad

I'm the fixer

I'm being honest

Please be happy

I must make people happy

I can't let them be sad

They must be happy around me

If not, I'll feel bad

My job is to fix

The problems in the world

If people aren't happy

That'd mean I've failed

I am made for this

I cannot fail

Making people happy

I must prevail

I control everything

That's how I want it to be

I am not real

I am imaginary

I am but a symbol

But a symbol of what?

A symbol of the worst feeling in the world

I can't control everything

I can't control anything

I can't make people

I'm not even happy

But my heart and brain are fighting

I'm happy

But I shouldn't need others to be.

So They Are Called

Every day I wonder

Who's next?

My misplaced trust

Leaves me perplexed

Who, of all my so-called friends,

Will leave me vexed

Who, I dare to ask,

Is next?

Who will play the next joke

that goes too far across the line

Who among these so-called friends of mine

Will dance on that line, so fine?

Who will make a comment,

that rips my heart in half?

Who, of all my so-called friends,

Will, through my heart, strike a gaff?

Who's next to linger

Heavy in my mind

To whose jokes will I be tethered

Who's next to cross my line?

I screamed today

Not out to anyone,

Into the sheets of my bed

Even though it seems cliche,

I screamed simply to scream

In a sad attempt to scare the pain away.

I wished it was a dream

An unconscious reality complexed.

But from this dream, that's not a dream,

I wake still wondering who's next.

I've prayed to find the ones

I've prayed for this to end

How much longer shall I be left to fend

This problem has been too long flexed

Who, I wonder, will be next?

Change Your Mind

A lot and a little at the same time

Like a poem or song without a rhyme

Sometimes I wonder what goes on in my own mind

yet peer inside, I do not, fearing what I might find.

So I look on, in the view of an onlooker

Seeing as much as an outsider could

Though on the outside

Never on the inside

In fear of what I might find

In fear of my own mind

Fear isn't something one is born into the world with,

But something that is taught,

Like literacy or walking stride

But the same way one is taught to handle pride.

I never feared my mind

I thought it was beautiful

Something I'd never have to hide

Something sensational

Remarkable

Impressive

And Important

Oh so important.

But to whom?

Me?

34

My friends?

My family?

After middle school,

I learned just how important

My mind could really be

Important, that is, to nobody.

People didn't like my thoughts

So why should I?

People used jealousy to dignify taunts

So why should I?

People that were supposed to love me

Ruined my own love for what I was good at

The one thing I loved to flaunt

And even now I can hear their haunts

But back then I gave no response.

I will respond now.

Why should I?

Why should I hide my mind?

It's beautiful!

It pours out wonderful things

So why should I still need people to tell me

Whether or not my thoughts mean something

To anybody.

My mind means everything

To me

People who disagree are nothing

To me.

Compared to them, my mind

Is useful for many things.

And I don't need them to tell me anything.

Countdown of The Days

How long, I wonder

Until you realize

That I'm too much

For you.

I count down the days

Until you finally see

And you get up and leave

And keep away from me.

Because I'm annoying

And I never leave you be

How long now

Until you're tired of me?

On that dreadful day

That you go away

I won't be okay

I'll cry and beg for you to stay

But even my plea is too much

And you'll leave anyway.

Then I'll move on

To the next people

Who are bound to hate me

When they see.

Sometimes I'm too much for me.

Finally

I found the people

That truly care

They listen and laugh

Rude remarks, they spare

How long until

I'm too much for them to bear?

I count down the days

Until it'll happen

And they'll leave

The story ends.

On that dreadful day

I won't be okay

I'll beg them to stay

And stay they may

But I can't get my hopes up

I must expect dismay

Because I'm too much for me

But if I was them, I would stay.

I am too much

But I am good.

I do everything right,

Just as I should.

But somehow I still

Worry about them

When will they

Get tired?

When will the story end

Once again?

Arachnophobia

When someone sees a spider

It's instinct to kill

Because it makes you feel scared

So death is the appeal

Step on the spider

To crush the fear away

Dead is the spider

Fear has gone astray.

The spider did nothing

But cause a little spook.

So why do we kill?

Just for it's look?

Spiders are scary

But the feeling doesn't justify

A murder.

It's just a spider

That makes us feel scared

So we attack with all we have

For war we are prepared.

All because we are scared.

The spider is scared too

For we are much bigger.

So it has defenses

that are automatically triggered.

The big ones can hiss

The little ones can jump

All of them can bite

But none of them stand a chance

against something else that is scared.

If the spider is big enough

We bring guns into the mix

But the guns are too much

And the spiders stand no chance

For they are just spiders

It's just a spider

And we're just people,

That are scared of an unseen evil.

Waterboarding

Out and about

The world around is loud

I often find it better

To be away from a crowd

Tuning out people Isn't

easy for me Sometimes

I wish They'd just leave

me be

But pushing them away,

Would be ignoring my longing

I wish for them to stay

44

So very contradicting

The people in my life
Serve as distractions
Distract me from my thoughts
Prevent my panicked actions

But at the same time
They fuel my thoughts
They hate me and I know it
However, I know not.

My thoughts hold me above water
Staring into the ocean-blue
The more my thoughts get to me
The deeper my head is pushed through.

My thoughts have a grasp on my hair
Tight, firm, strong

They'll never let go

As my head is shoved deeper.

The water fills my lungs

Yet I can still breathe

My thoughts won't let me die

It's more fun to watch me heave.

No one cares

I should just leave

No one cares

About me.

I'm coughing up water

I've washed up on the beach

It seems my thoughts

Might let me sleep.

I stare up at the sky

Pause for a moment

Then back at the water

Why?

My thoughts sit before me now

Heaving their own breaths

They do not control me for now

It appears they're letting me rest

They look tired

Tired as I

I want to hurt them

I have reasons why

They hurt me

So why shouldn't I?

But they don't deserve it

They've been through as much as I

It's my own fault

For believing every lie

People care about me

People love me

I have my reasons not to trust people

Yet I have no reason to push them from me.

It's my own fault

It's my mistake

I know my thoughts are liars

Why do I listen?

They're so loud

But this beach is quiet

I only see it sometimes

When my thoughts let me sleep

The water is calm

The water is clear

And if I close my eyes

I can actually hear

The people that are around me

Do I really deserve them?

I can't believe they found me

While I'm deserted by the ocean

I can hear them

They're happy to be around me

With me

Beside me.

I know that they're not lying to me.

My thoughts hold me above water

They tell me it's not true

They notice every

Detail

Every side glance

Every half smile

Every sigh

Every sign of my friends' unhappiness

"They hide it in their smile"

I say

"It's my fault"

I say

As my head is shoved down under

I am not okay

Because my thoughts won't be quiet

This beach is quiet

I'm coughing up water

My head hovers over the ocean blue and vast

How long will my thoughts keep their grasp?

The Ignorance of a Child

I wonder what children think

About the problems of the world.

Do they care?

Do they know?

Childlike wonder,

Is something that's destroyed

When the world makes contact

It's left to the void.

Where does it go?

It's passed on to the children's children

To protect them

And keep them out of the know.

Temporarily, unfortunately.

Eventually, they'll discover

What their parents cover.

Then what's left of their childlike wonder?

The ignorance of a child.

They don't know of trouble.

But they will find out soon

That the world is wild,

That people hide pain with fake smiles.

The loss of innocence due to ignorance

The ignorance of a child.

Betrayal

What is betrayal?

Is it when the hero prevails?

And gives the hero ails.

Many believe betrayal is when

The hero is stabbed in the back by the villain

However what most don't realize,

is that betrayal never comes from the bad guy.

After all

To be betrayed

You have to trust

54

The one who swayed

Your trust

And made you believe

That they'd never leave.

Until they do leave

A knife in your back

Sticking out

Visible

Betrayal isn't trivial

It's simply, easy

But unbelievable.

"But it's not easy!"

Really?

Is it so difficult that you choose them over me?

So hard that you can't stay true to me?

So straining that you have to hurt me?

If it's so difficult then show what you're feeling.

I know that you don't care.

If you did,

What's this disloyalty?

You obviously don't care

So go on, betray me.

I don't care either

I'm not sad

Why should I be?

It's not all your fault that I've stopped trusting.

So go on, betray me

Take what little trust I have left

Rip it apart

You might as well take my heart

As well

After all, you don't care

I have failed

Against the villain, my friend

What is betrayal?

Something that will never end.

Fake Pain

When thinking of pain

We think of something physical

Like a wound

Or maybe something more trivial.

Like a toothache

Or a headache

Or a muscle ache

Or a bone break

But doctors don't often account

For what most believe is fake.

Physical pain can be described

as an ache, a burn; it can be cried

but for some ailments, doctors cant provide

for something "fake", they can't prescribe.

Ironically this "fake" pain

hurts more than any cut or sprain.

it can't be diagnosed, explained, or described

It's not visible externally

it's felt on the inside.

It tears through your organs,

body, and soul.

Leaving a hole,

gaping, open wide,

never seen on the outside.

so it can't be real

and it cant be treated

so this illness easily kills

victims are cheated.

When thinking of pain

Don't just think physical

think of the "fake"

and struggle to explain.

Think of the miserable, untreatable pain.

Now think of how many are called "insane".

I do wonder

what goes on in one's brain.

But I'm no doctor

So I guess it's all the same

oh, what a shame.

Looking in the Glass Case

There's an empty art exhibit

with my name on it

plastered on a gold shining plaque

with dark hardwood as the back

etched into the glimmer

my name clearly shows

in this empty art exhibit

that nobody knows

it's built for me

an architectural beauty

and it stands in the center

and it is empty

I think it explains me.

nothing but air
to look at in there
nothing to see
I think it explains me.

this empty art exhibit
that was built just for me
standing in a museum somewhere
filled with just air
It explains me.

There's an empty art exhibit
with my name on it
plastered in a gold shining plaque

and there's nothing else to it

nothing in the fine print

yet there's nothing

that it lacks.

It explains me.

at least what I'm feeling

this art exhibit

is empty

there's an empty art exhibit

and I'm standing in it

yet still it's not filled

it's empty

I remain still

It is for me.

Behind Brown Eyes

A river rushes

the water is cold

and salty

it's faulty

like a faucet

that's lost it

the water pressure

pushed it

yet not a droplet shows

behind the walls of iron

behind the color brown

behind the deep frown

fix the dam

but fixing means fixing

repairing, rebuilding

but this dam is ever so

limiting.

so fixing means a hammer and

explosives, detonation. destroy

every brick in that dam let the

water fall, rush, flow

behind the walls of iron

it aches to get out

itching at the color brown

no such thing as a frown

a frown is just a smile

that is upside down.

the dam has been broken for a while

but the water won't fall down.

so now we keep damaging the dam

in hopes that the water will flow

but the damage isn't necessary

the damage hurts the wall

but the water won't flow

so the water over-fills

and it slowly kills

the island

because if the island can't release the water

then the island is in danger.

The island slowly sinks

but water may flow soon

after all the damage

is soon going to be enough

and the dam will break.

When Your Eyes Met Mine

Meeting at the place with the bittersweet smell

unknowing of each other's personal hell

but you turned your head when I walked in

something told you you might as well.

why did your eyes shine like gold

when you met mine so dull?

So forgotten?

why did they light up in awe?

And I thought, you're gorgeous

there's no chance you'd be looking at me.

67

Im a miserable sight to see

but you...

You are the beauty found in darkness

just like the reason people enjoy the night sky

the enigmatic essence of your being

has managed to make me ask why.

Why are you looking at me?

After all I've done

I don't deserve it

but please don't point your glance elsewhere

because I need it.

For some reason

it pumps life through my veins

It takes away my pain

for but just one second...

until you look away.

and I am lost again.

Anywhere but Home

I'm still sitting

at my desk at home

waiting to be instructed

waiting to be told

I'm not anywhere but there

not anywhere but home.

I'm still eating macaroni and cheese

on the couch

while you sleep

right next to me.

I'm not anywhere but there

not anywhere but home.

I'm not gonna grow up
I'm not gonna lose myself on a journey
I'm not gonna leave just yet
I dont think I'm quite ready

So I'm gonna stay here
right where I belong
I'm not going anywhere
anywhere but home.

I'm still learning how to
play soccer you're there
teaching standing right
beside me

I'm still watching
that show on tv

71

the one that you love

to watch with me

And I wish this didn't happen so fast

and I miss when moments lasted

and life didn't happen this quickly

It's all got me feeling sickly.

So I'm still in bed

with a high fever

falling asleep

fever dream

and when I wake up

I'm still in high school

graduating soon

And I could go anywhere

But right now I want to be home.

Clock That's Also a Bomb

These moments we cherish

are starting to seem rare

It seems like I never have

enough time

Even though I have the rest of my life.

I long for those moments

where I can rest on your chest

and breathe easy

and soak up the memory.

But now I feel it fading and I

feel I am forsaking every free

moment I have left trying to

make the best

of my final year in high school.

But I'm worried sick

I'm so terrified.

I miss my family already

but I haven't left them behind.

Am I already gone?

Am I no longer a child?

Is it wrong for me to cry

and ask for my mother?

Is it still okay

that I need her hugs,

her reassuring words,

and her life-giving love?

College approaches,

yet I'm so far from adulthood

and I fear that's catching up with me.

It's odd to deal with college when you're fifteen

and my brain

is finally feeling the weight

and the pressure

it's explosive

I still have a year

but I feel it's already wasted.

There's so much I have to do

and so little time.

and I rarely find my family time on my mind.

so I'm losing my mind.

I feel so separated from them,

though we talk every day.

And I want to spend every last waking moment with them.

but my mind always keeps me busy.

and I hate myself for it

for putting my hobbies above my family

I don't know why I do it

it's not helping my problem

I miss them so much that I can't see

how much time I really have left.

I have a ton.

but it's as though it's already gone.

Because time moves like sound

swift and silent

but blinding and painful when you don't expect it.

When the Sun No Longer Shines
by the Moon's Side

Long before eternity

before the earth bore a tree

or grass or land or water

before the earth came to be

the sun and the moon

lived happily

in unison

in harmony

they shined side by side

bright and wide

close by

they'd never collide

The sun and moon
were the best of friends
never to leave
one another.

but soon the earth came about
and their lives became greater

for the sun and moon now served
the earth
and the heaven's
that may be above

and they were separate
but so important
in each of their
separate lives

79

never seeing each other

as one sets, the other will rise.

But together they'd cause the earth to fall

so even the sun and moon can't have it all.

two close friends

bond unbreakable

brought to the end

by fate, unshakable

rising,

setting,

orbiting.

Separate.

The sun found herself getting desperate

trying with might, while she watched the moon go

shining so bright

all on her own.

and it brought the sun joy

to see her friend so happy

but happy without her

shining brightly.

the sun worried for a while

that she outshined the moon

and worried that the moon might hate

her, as she was compared to.

but now the sun sees

that they are better off

as separate entities

shining for their own joy, shining separately

And the sun watches the moon

and wonders if the moon watches her back

she hopes the moon is proud of how she shines now

even if she's shining alone.

Long after eternity

when earth had people

earth had dreams

long after it came to be

the sun and moon

lived happily,

though separately

both shining ever so brightly.

Equation

I've always been better with words,

not numbers

beautiful works of literature

more than awful mathematical blunders

But even I,

the mathematics denier

know one plus one is two

and nothing more to

My problems starts

when X enters the equation

the desirable outcome

from number persuasion

one plus five equals X

X being the desirable outcome

but what happens when X is not desirable

When the outcome becomes the problem

One plus one

was easy enough

until one subtracted

then it got rough

One plus three

was also easy

almost two easy

one minus three

outcome X

comes out undesirably

One minus five

got a bit tricky

so many numbers

to account for

But the answer remains the same

scratch work is in vain

it always equals X

the answer will not change

That is until Y

makes its appearance

on the other side

of the equal sign remaining by one's side

even when the outcome is X

Now I'm starting to believe

Maybe math isn't that difficult.

To the People I Love |
On My Deathbed

If I was to die tomorrow

and knew of the inevitable

I wouldn't try to experience the world's wonders

and force the events that make life liveable

I wouldn't need to see the Eiffel Towers' glow

amidst the dirtied, worn streets of Paris

I wouldn't buy a plane ticket to Japan

though I've always wished to go

I wouldn't make amends

with anyone I've wronged

I wouldn't call my friends

and ask to sing one more song

In fact, If I was to die tomorrow

and knew what was to happen,

I would spend the day in my mother's arms, crying

though the action is unlively and mere

I'd seek her comfort because death is something I still
fear.

I'd tell her she'd done well

as my mother and my friend

I'd tell her not to worry

even if it is the end

I'd beg her not to cry

even with tears falling from my eyes

I can't stand to see her lose herself

when her daughter dies

I'd tell my other mother

that she's got to stay the same

and not to let this low point

affect her brain

I'd tell her that I love her so

and that she always does so much

They both do.

I'd tell her to take a break once in a while

even if she doesn't choose to.

And just to make sure she keeps the words in transit,

I'd finish my sentence with words that stuck with me

"I love you, don't ever forget it"

Then I'd ask them

to tell my little sister

that I went off to college

or did something cool

because as much as she argues with me

I know that she'd never be the same

If her sister died

so I'd plead with my mothers

Not to tell her

until she's older

and can handle it better.

and when the time comes

I'd tell them to relay

that I went out in a cool way

like going into space

or saving a snake

I know that she'd like that.

and if I wake up the next day

and I'm no longer in the realm of the living

I will make them know that I'm not gone yet

and I will never leave

because my fear is not death itself

but how the people I love will live on without me.

But my death is not soon

I'm not ready yet

I have many years ahead

before I wind up dead

this is just precautionary

perhaps even informational

When I die

I hope no one cries because I've spent my whole life
trying to make people happy.

So if I died tomorrow

I wouldn't do what everyone thinks

I would beg my family to stay the same

and carry on

the last thing I'd want to do with my death,

is disrupt my family's life.

and I probably wouldn't be able to say these words at
the time

I'd just cry and tell them I love them every second of my
final day

because as it turns out,

even if my country is falling to bad hands

even if the world is burning slowly

I still don't want to go away.

So I'd ask the people I love to live on in my name.

Pledge

I pledge allegiance

to the flag

that stands for freedom

in this land

but not the flag

that I see now

tainted by

American sorrow

It's illegal to burn the flag

but it's already ablaze

not with praise

not in the good way

torn down

ripped, burned

vandalized

by America's hurtful crimes

Leave it to America

to change the meaning of a word

freedom is no long free

liberty is controlled

It's odd to think

how illness arrived and wiped out the old

now the young are being raised

and young minds listen to what they're told

America promotes freedom

life of liberty

but life where no one can be different

that's the new meaning of free

Under God? indivisible?

We're more divided than ever

people are dying

from discrimination

division is all

that's become of our nation.

Gay people

White people

Straight people

Black People

the only thing that's undivided among that

is that we're all people

And that's all we should see.

America undivided?

We're all people

But some don't know how to treat others

This is why other countries mock us

because of our "liberty"

Why is this happening?

because that's what they're teaching

what America is promoting

It's not just the voting.

Whoever becomes president

doesn't matter.

Our free country

has been irreversibly tattered.

I'm pledging allegiance

to the government

because the flag clearly no longer matters

congratulations, country of liberty

we are officially

completely shattered

We can try picking up the pieces

and gluing it together

but the damage is irreparable

because people are stubborn creatures

once they believe something

it's impossible to change their minds

so that's why people die

from the most common illness,

not the flu, not covid

hatred.

America is a zoo

people are the animals

the government is the keepers

and they're doing poorly

they don't treat fleas

the fleas spread rapidly

flea infected animals

hatred infected humans

both scared and in pain

then they start to hurt others

if people opened their eyes

and thought for themselves

Maybe we could piece the

pieces back together

but that will never happen

so America continues to wither.

Water | Gas

Water gas

I never asked

for the burns on my hands

and my heart

They scarred nicely

so everyone could see them

and know that I'm vulnerable

to the heat

Air water,

hot steam

I inhaled it.

It almost choked me

to death

I hated its

burning heat

but somehow I survived

only burned severely

and it hurt for such a long time

but now I can barely feel it.

Because it turns out

steam fades away

with time and effort

and meeting new people

The scars are still there

but someone cares now

unlike you did

I'm better now.

How are you?

Are you a better person?

Are you less of an exasperation?

Water Gas.

Water | Solid

Water solid.

Can I even call it

water any longer?

it's just ice

Cold, uncomfortable,

even harmful.

I have to be so careful

if I drop it I could break it

Comfortable for a while

but soon just cold

and lonely

freezing me only

I thought I could last

but I only ended up losing a finger

a limb

and almost my nose To

the unreliable

unbearable, freezing cold

and I curse you

for hurting me

but you never meant to,

right?

You're just cold by nature...

Frozen water, ice.

But I got tired

of tiptoeing in the freezing cold

quite quickly,

it got old

For ice is uncomfortable,

fragile, and frigid.

Cold is painful, but not detrimental,

Water solid.

Water | Free

Water Free.

Flowing beautifully.

Only you can read my mind

Every word, all the time

I don't have to be careful

of getting burned or frozen

because you'd never hurt me

like those in the past

I never have to try

I always wonder why

you stick around, like hot weather in the most
southern state of those United.

but I do often worry that I may drown

a soul so deep and wonderful

like an ocean grand and profound

but with an uncrowded beach

just silence and peace

and that's what's so scary.

I know you'll never leave me

but what if I do something?

what if I mess up

and your calm water becomes, too, tainted?

I've messed up many times

oil spilling in

turning the beautiful water black from its wonderful
blue

I really don't want that to happen to you.

My closest friend

Calm quiet blue

I really don't know

what to do

I've lost so much.

So many times

so maybe that's why

I find it odd

that you're so kind

flowing beautifully,

Water free.

Marmata Monax

How much wood would a woodchuck chuck if a
woodchuck could chuck wood?

How many friends could one person lose

if one should choose to try and be herself

even with no luck

that must suck

every day try the same way

to please all the people she wants to befriend

it always ends with her out of luck,

stuck in the endless cycle of thinking she'll never be
enough

How much wood would a woodchuck chuck

when one girl thinks that she is shuck

forsaken by everyone,

never apart of the ruck.

When her kindness is slowly plucked from her person

always mistaken with her judge of character

always forsaken, never having any fun

how much wood would a woodchuck chuck

if one girl is finally done?

How much wood could a woodchuck chuck

if one girl doesn't care

if a woodchuck could chuck wood

wouldn't it be weird?

because woodchucks aren't supposed to chuck wood.

and not all friends are supposed to stay friends.

Time passes much too quickly

and relationships end almost abruptly

How many friends could one person lose...

a lot, you'd be surprised

at the amount of tears that have left my eyes

over something that doesn't matter.

because relationships can be replaced or revised

and experience and time only make them better.

Over It:

Are you really over it

when it still lingers in your mind

you've truly gotten over it

but are you really fine?

Are you really over it

when everything reminds you

and the thought still seems to find you

so are you really fine

Are you really over it when

you still bring it up when you

want people to talk You're

not really fine

You're still throwing a fit

there's no way you could be over it.

Are you really over it

when the thoughts are still there

messing up your hair

it's never fair

is it?

Because you'll never be over it.

P.A.R.A.N.O.I.A

Persistently looking everywhere

All at once, in fear

Regrets plague my mind

And I cannot rest to save my life

Nothing is there

Only my overactive

Imagination, making me think things

Are not okay

Desperate to fall asleep but

Imaginary fears keep me from

Slumber, I wonder why.

Thoughts provoked by nothing

Racing through my brain

Always driving me insane

Consciousness starts to wane

Troubling and true

Exation ensues

Distracted, my thoughts refracted.

Please make this stop

All of this must stop I'm

Reaching the point of insanity, losing my

Astuteness, a mental calamity.

Never couldn't thought that

Overthinking could destroy me

Indefinitely, broken

Always worrying

Longing to gain control of my

Overestimations, begging for

Oasis, freedom, peace, free from

Knowledge and destruction

But I'll never escape the

Exuberant mental quakes

Haunted forever by something

Imagined by the brain, completely fake.

Nothing I can do to

Dissipate this feeling

Mentally, I am

Exhausted.

Persistently looking everywhere

Around me and behind me,

Right and left of me

All the time.

Never stopping, thinking

Overtime.

Intellectual, and mental state

Destroyed, that's my fate.

Insufferable constant

Sequences of pain

Mind tricks and gimmicks

Energy wanes

The White Room

I woke up in a room

With walls white like snow

Others were there to

Others I didn't know

"Where am I?"

I asked a girl with black hair

She didn't look at me when she spoke

Her voice laced with despair

I was rather confused by her reply

She said,

"You're in the room,

The room of white."

She wasn't wrong

The room was white

Whiter than the clouds

That plaster the sky

"I suppose you're right."

I responded,

"This room is white."

She nodded.

Her answer was clear,

correct, and nice

But it's not what I was looking for,

So I looked to someone else for advice.

There was a boy with blonde hair

and round brown eyes.

"Hello sir," I said,

"Are you someone in which I can confide?"

He nodded,

"What is it that you need?"

"Where am I and why?"

I asked.

He quickly replied,

"You're in the room of white."

Now I was getting miffed.

"This room is very white,

But there's something else.

What is it?"

"It's small,"

he said.

"That's all," he said

"That you're missing."

He wasn't wrong.

The room was small.

Very small,

Cramped, and controllable.

"Why am I here?" I asked him.

He said, "If you're in the room of white,

There's always a reason

No one gets sent to the tight room of white

When they've got no right to be here."

Then I saw a window.

I don't know how I missed it.

It was bright and obvious.

And people were outside it.

"And what of the people out there?"

I pointed through the window.

"They are not allowed in here.

The room of white is for us alone."

I didn't like talking to the boy with blonde hair

He seemed to handle advice with no care.

So I said,

"Goodbye, sir, I'm going elsewhere."

Then I walked to the window

And peered outside.

The world there was vast and wide.

And I'd been there before, but I couldn't remember it.

And a girl walked by

And she acted as though she couldn't see me

Or anybody

In the room of white

Then I was struck

With a thought of remembrance

"I know her"

I thought.

So I hit the window

Hard and loud.

But she kept walking,

Unbothered.

"She can't see you."

Someone uttered.

I didn't care to listen

To the spouting of arrogant words.

Of course, she could see me

She was right there.

I hit the window again.

Still no reaction.

"You don't understand,

You're pointless with your actions".

That person again.

Telling me lies.

"Why can't she see me?"

I finally asked.

"You see they only see what

They want to see...

Those people outside of the room of white,

Who think they're always right."

"What?"

I asked.

But then there was no one.

And I was alone there with the window.

And she was right there

On the other side of the white room.

The words I was told made me wonder
Who's truly not allowed where?

Are they not allowed in?
Or are we not allowed out?

"I want out!" I screamed.

And then I was there.
In my old room.
And grew to fear
The white room.

But slowly,
Living in that world,
The color drifted away.

And became white, and cold.

The white room slowly

Became my world.

And people still saw me.

But it wasn't the real me.

Just a shell

That they chose to see.

So I searched for that window that I'd seen before.

And I stood on the other side, crying.

"Let me back in,"

I said.

And then I was there.

And the room of white

Was not as bare.

In fact, it felt more like home

Than the other world

That I was trapped in.

Turns out,

No one wants to live in a world

That they're not allowed to be in.

It's Raining

There's a feeling no one can capture

Lest the vocals turn to rapture

Screams and cries are all that explain

The indubitably awful exerberant pain

On this night I listen to the rain

And I mark my thoughts down as those insane

Wondering if having a brain is in vain

Lest we don't experience the unexplained pain

Like a glass frame shattered

Blocking the view of art

None can see this feeling

That tears the soul apart

Unseen and unheard of

Unexplained and unkept

Many a night I have stayed later and later

Many a night I have wept

Many a night the feeling grows greater

Many a night I could have slept

Oh the awful feeling that one cannot capture

I fear it's beginning to reflect on my stature

The bags under my eyes, the scars on my mind

And the presence of this damned feeling

Perhaps I should resign

All my life I've tried to explain

That which can only be by screaming

And crying and lurching and grabbing one's hair

Pulling it out while other people stare.

Laughing out loud after, like you didn't care

But dying inside there

Because how is it fair

To be plagued with a feeling

That's unnamed a feeling.

Oh, the shame to try and explain

Something so out of reach and vague

Yet so incredibly

Sporadic and amazed

That one look from a human eye

Could turn them about enraged

And they'd never be the same

When locked in a cage,

And perhaps that's what it is

Bars of thoughts

Trapping us in the rusting corners

By the borders

Of actual sanity

Maybe we control the calamity

This feeling we can't explain

It's a need

Carnal and freeing

But away it's eating

At every essence of being

So very discomforting

If only we knew what call it by

A name, a face, a bright blue sky

A ribbon of DNA buried in our blood

Perhaps it's something that can never be gone for good.

I Have Plans

I have plans today

I'm excited for them

I've written them on my calendar

I'm ready to execute them

I had plans today

But they were pushed back

They're not happening today

And that's okay

I have a headache today

I don't know why

I also feel as if

I should start to cry

I have plans again soon

Something to look forward too

However so much to do

Before my plans ensue.

And I have a headache.

I have plans

But I can't see them

All I can see is a task at hand

Smothering me

Bothering me

Ensuring that nothing is enjoyable

Until finally,

I have plans again

This weekend

131

I can't wait

For them

To begin

I sure hope

Nothing happens

My plans finally happened

It was fun while it lasted

Now I have nothing

Nothing but the mounds of responsibilities

And nothing to look forward to

Nothing that I can see.

So I lay, stressed in wait

For the day that finally

I have plans again

Not with anyone,

Just by myself

I'm excited

My plans couldn't happen

Because I'm so behind

Ahead of the class

But behind sitting on my ass

Because I have nothing to look forward to

So why bother moving forward?

So I'll stay stagnant until that feeling descends

And I have plans once again.

I'm so tired.

A poetic dance on the fine line of nothing:

I often find myself in a poetic mood

When I'm searching for something to be happy about

When I'm lying in bed late at night

Too late to be awake

And I stare at my unmoving fan

Desperate to sleep while my brain fades

In and out of the thoughts

Weaving all around to find

Something to be happy about

It's an empty feeling

One that cannot be described with words

That are different than

The single word "poetic"

Artists find inspiration from natural scenery

Poets do as well

A natural scenery visible to only us

In our terrifying minds that work

Only when emptied by the lack of presence

Of something to be happy about.

This poetic feeling

This place I'm in

Staring at my bare unmoving ceiling

Lasts for a while each night

And it eats away at my mind

Until I'm finally tired enough to pass out.

And on this night,

Quiet as most

In my dark room

I'm engulfed with the feeling

And I have a thought

That I haven't written in a while.

And perhaps that's why this poetic feeling

Has been taking me over

More often

These days in recent.

I hope after this

I'll finally feel decent.

Perhaps this poetic problem

Comes only when one is void of emotions

And therefore has nothing to put

Onto a paper or into a document

But why can I not write of nothing at all?

When nothing is the most common thought.

Perhaps that is because of the fine line

That exists between everything and nothing.

That is the line which poets feel the need

To lie next to

As if measuring their height

Along the universal line

I like to dance on it

As an elegant ballerina of theoretical artistry

Hire me if thou seeks

A talented dancer as I

One that can dance on a line of thought

So finely

But one that can never seem to distinguish between

Everything and nothing.

And thus the return

Of the sad poetic feeling.

The dreadful feeling

of everything meaning absolutely nothing.

Everything is too much

Nothing is too little

Everything is vibrant and blinding

But nothing is far too bare

Everything is loud

Nothing is too quiet

When everything is nothing

Is that not the perfect balance?

A diet of all that one needs

Everything, nothing.

I'm going to return to that poetic feeling

And continue to stare at my ceiling

And maybe then I'll drift off to sleep

And with that, I've found something to be

Happy about.

Narcissistic Champaign Bottle Pop, On the Roof Top of a Skyscraper

Congratulations

Because you made it

Might as well

Celebrate it

It was tough

And seemed impossible

But you did it

Anyways

Now look at all those who doubted you

And say to them

How much you've laughed at them

For how wrong they were

Because guess what,

I was never too young for anything

I was never not mature.

Never not seeing

Anything differently

From how an adult would see.

And people might've misjudged me,

underestimated me,

Or straight up ignored me

When my ideas were strong

Just because I'm young

Does that make my ideas wrong?

Guess what,

It doesn't

And it never did

And it never will no matter how young I am

In any situation

I'll always be older,

Mentally older

More mature, colder

Bolder, with the ability

To shoulder anything thrown at me.

And life has thrown so much at me

Too much for a young girl.

But I relish it

And ask for more.

Hit me with everything

I'll bear it so others don't have to.

My mind can take it

Because it's what I was made for.

So keep on misplacing me with the younger crowd.

And watch my self-worth shy away

At the fact that I am always

Underestimated because of my age.

So congratulations to me

For making it this far

Without being clinically insane,

Diagnosed at least.

And hats off to me

For dealing with the bullshit of everybody

That seemed to think

They could take me to the brink

Of my own self-aware

Mental state.

And they tried to fill me with so much hate.

But they also underestimated

The fact that I turn hate into

Something great.

Something magnificent,

worth celebrating.

So hoo-rah to me

And yippee-kai-ay

Because I'm going to take it one day

Further

And tackle my dreams

Even better.

And I'll stand at the very top,

In my cleared-out spot

That I've been decorating and preparing

Since my early childhood

When I decided

That being young was never going to stop me

From going, and getting

And always achieving

And never grieving over the people

Who said I was nothing.

So I'm at the top

Of my self-proclaimed sky-scraper

Push me down if you want!

But you can't because it's wrong to hit a child.

And that's what you've considered me all along

So why is it any different when I'm at the top?

Perhaps it was jealousy all along

That made you use your words to try and stop me.

But how did that work out?

I'd assume poorly.

So three cheers for me

As insufferable as I may be

Because I worked for everything

That I hold in my hand now

And I'll be damned if someone

Try's to imply that I didn't

Die a million times over

Just to stand at the top of my

Theoretical sky-scraper.

I want to hear

The cheers of my name

Not from the followers of my fame

But from the faces of those who never believed in the
young girl who was in their life.

The young girl who just wanted friends

and support

and love.

The young girl who thought she could tackle the world

but found that people were much more difficult.

It's weird to think about and kind of sad

That people are the only thing that I truly allowed
myself to fail at.

So maybe I don't need their cheers.

Maybe I don't need any.

No, I have plenty.

Just the view is enough.

From the very top, you can't get one any better.

And when the hard work pays off,

It's the best feeling ever.

And when you finally know that everything you've
dreamed of your entire life

Now seems so easy.

Life seems so peaceful

And I feel the need to congratulate me.

Lesson Plan For Life

I started high school younger than most

but never worried about the workload

I worried about how my class would perceive

the new younger girl in their ranks

The work, it was easy

planned accordingly

by each day

a lesson plan to lead the way

I knew I could follow it

and everything would be okay

But there wasn't plan

for how to talk to them.

We all entered freshmen year

not knowing anything

we were at the bottom of the social food chain

we had to start over again.

And the lessons,

they were easy

for the entire student body

but people aren't planned out based on a formula.

So tell me teacher

Tell me someone

cuz I'm struggling

to understand.

Where's the plan

for how to

talk to them?

Tell me teacher
I need a tutor

social problems worse than those in math
the hardest work, and there's no lesson plan for that.

And junior year
it was the hardest
workload doubled
prepare for college

and maintain
sports and spirits too
along with your
friend group

And applications
they're not hard to fill out
not at all

what's bad is that our motivation's fall

they plument down and leave us alone.

So tell me teacher

tell me someone

what am I supposed

to do

Tell me teacher

tell me someone

There's nothing

that I want to do

and soon I'll be a grad

I need to get my motivation back

So tell me teacher where's the lesson plan for that?

And in about seventy days

we'll walk across that stage.

and that's it

that life after high school,

we'll be living it.

As unprepared

as a teenager

can get.

Not ready for the brute force of the worlds'

pain and strife.

Tell me, teacher, Tell

me someone Where's

the lesson plan for life?

Someday, Yesterday, Today, and a Year From Now:

Someday I'll be famous among many

Known as an author, as a poet to most any

In that grand hard-earned chair I will have sat

But I have a few more years before that

Someday I'll stand on a big wide stage

Overlooking everyone at my age

Wearing a robe and a matching hat

But I have a few more years before that

Someday I'll start

Where I never thought

And make friends for a lifetime yet

But I have a few years before that

Someday I'll leave class

Never to return

Only to show that I learn better fast

But I have a few years before that

Someday I'll say I'm better than others

And stand above those who don't know shapes and colors

In triumph and stat

But I have a few years before that

Someday I'll take my very first steps

Speak my very first words

And know nothing of the world

Around me

155

Present, future, past

I still have a few more years before that

Next year I turn seventeen

And I'm scared of what will come to be

I look back on my life, it's been long and good

But not long enough, to worry where I'm at

I have many more years to do that.

Say Goodbye:

Tie me to a pole

And walk away with no regret

And I'll sit in the rain

And not know what's even happening

But I'm gonna miss you more than

I even know what missing people is

When I see you on the street

While I'm wandering

I'll walk up to you not knowing

Not caring about the damage I'll cause to myself

The time was golden

But fools watch it rust

Because even the best moments

Must be left in the dust

Of life

That moves too quickly

And I'll miss you

More than I even know the meaning of missing

I'll never sit in that car

I'll never sing that song

I'll never touch the grass

Without wondering how you're doing

When, if we meet again

Let the moments shine

Through the coat of dust

They'll collect over time

So we can laugh about

The days where everything

Was okay

And we were together

But now we're going to stand in the rain

And walk away

Not because we want to

But because we have to

To move on with the course

Of the life

That destroys

And creates epiphany's of joy

And sadness

And constructs time in it's essence

The most important thing

Is that I'll miss you more than I can miss anything.

I'll miss this

More than I can say.

Song of the Fauna

Red and white

Blood on the snow

There's no place to go

Wildlife around

Can't notice me

While I sit and freeze

And all I can think

While I'm brought to the brink of life

Is how it's so peacefully quiet.

And then I hear the animals sing

162

"There's no rest for the wicked

But you sit in the frigid

And slow as it may be,

You will rest, for you are kind."

And I pay their song no piece of mind.

This is a distant land

There is no way I could understand

Their beautiful language

Slowly my mind freezes with my body

And I wonder if this is the most

At ease I've felt in a while

Such a great feeling

Yet I'm too cold to smile

Then the animals gather round

To sing the next chorus

"Do not fret

It is your time

Blissfully sleep

For you are kind"

And I pay their song no mind

As I freeze to death in the land on the line

Hate is a Strong Word

How could you hate me?

Why wouldn't you?

I know everything that I do

You think is to annoy you

But I suppose

that's true for me too.

And I can't see in your mind.

Why do you hate me?

I'll never know why

So I'll look to the sky

With a silent prayer

Even if I don't believe in any deity out there

I'll scream, I'll attract all the stares

What did I do to make you

Hate me so much, it consumes you?

And I allow myself to get annoyed

With everything you do

And it's a bad habit

With which I've wasted my time

And I wish I could tell you why

Because you deserve that much.

But maybe it really is just because

We were meant to be enemies

But we're born in proximity

If there really is a deity, they sure have a sense of humor.

I'm sure, to you, I've felt like a tumor

Slowly driving you crazy with my presence

I'm sorry that the very essence

of my being disturbes you so.

And it saddens me that, in terms of understanding each other...

We've got too long a way to go.

But I've tried.

So very hard.

To get you to talk to me.

But you look at me with a smile, telling me you think it's funny.

But then I hear you cry in the shower,

Screaming that you hate me.

The Created

What should I do

You've instructed me with every part of my being

What should I do

To ensure that you stay by my side?

I used to be a plethora of colors

My own accord

Until you showed up and

Washed everything on my palette away

You made me a blank canvas

So that I'd hand you the paintbrush

So you'd take it

And paint my personality

Exactly how you wanted it to be.

And you painted with colors

That I would never choose

To lay upon myself

Willingly

But with your guidance,

I practically grabbed the brush myself

And drew up a new life

In your name

One that you got a say in

But you weren't mother nature

You weren't my creator

But you softly laid the paintbrush

Upon my skin

And everything that you wanted

Was what I became

And of all the colors

You painted red

And blue, and black, and purple

All across my face and my body

Painting my new life

Without my consult

Or my consent

But you didn't need to know that you didn't have it.

Because you had everything

Everything I gave to you.

Then when you finally left

And found a prettier painting

To ruin

I was left a mosaic of bruises and emotions

Colors that I never wanted anyone to see.

So I grabbed the white paint

And I took it upon myself

To cover everything

So no one could see how much I was hurting.

Then you showed up again

With a bucket of water

And you "cleansed" me

Of the hiding

You took the liberty

Of revealing everything.

So after that,

I tried to scrape the paint from my canvas

It hurt so much

But no one ever knew

Then your artistry was fully removed

But the pain remained

Permanently stained into my skin

A painful reminder of the awful paintbrush you

Forced upon my skin

With promises of a beautiful product

That isn't what happened.

Now I'm a mess

A masterpiece no one wishes to buy

Unless, once again,

I paint myself white

And I hide

The Tears We've Cried

I don't want to exist with people's problems anymore.

Is it too much to just wish for existence?

Just existence.

I don't want any obligations,

I don't wish to fall forever.

I want to stop seeing sad faces

and stop falling.

I hate being blamed for every single problem in people's lives.

"Sorry, I was crying"

"Stop you made me cry!"

"No! Please don't cry!"

The places I've seen,

the people I've interacted with...

I don't want them to be sad anymore.

But they're always sad when I see them.

For I am nothing more

than an aid to people's ailments.

Not good enough to be a cure

and not bad enough to be a problem.

So I'll fall forever

Until people learn how to solve them

Freefall

I'll fall with you

Even as the heavens and the earth fall with me

Even as my mind separates from my body

I'll fall with you

I'll climb the height

By my own accord

Even with damage

That I can't afford

Then I'll slip and reach for your hand

You'll extend though far from it

I'll try to hold on, reaching far

Then I'll fall to the summit

I'll lie there on the floor

Broken and cold

Because even as your antics

Are getting old

I can't let go of them

I'll never have control of them

And I'll always be

On the receiving end

You haven't fallen yet

But you'll be down here soon

You need to pick me up again, get me on my feet

Balance me out and promise me things so the process
can repeat.

Snow falls on the mountain

From the sky blue

I take a moment to wonder

Is cold for you too?

They weren't lying when they said winter was the coldest season

I wish fate was real so I could say this happened for a reason

And I look to the sky every time I feel like crying

Hoping something falls in my eye and gives me time to feel some other pain

Besides resentment towards your name

And God I hate you so much

But I can't stop screaming for you to look my way.

You breath life into my body

Only when you can breathe

Because you're falling too

You're starting to heave

The air in your lungs

Is starting to leave

You're falling from that height

Falling with me

About the Author:

My name is Riley Goldberg, I'm a sixteen year-old senior in highschool and a sophomore in college via duel enrollment. I was homeschooled for most of my life due to bullying in early elementary school. After that I advanced my schooling exponentially. I didn't have many friends so instead of relaxing over summer break, I would just start the next school grade. That's how I got to where I am now. Over this time I've struggled with severe anxiety and, in the recent years, depression as well as some other disorders that could be seen as "hindering" however, I apply them to the studies of my field and produce works that hopefully others can relate to.

Made in United States
Troutdale, OR
02/24/2024

17953725R00104